Our Weather & Water

Teacher Supplement

1:1
Answers
IN GENESIS™

GOD'S
DESIGN®

4th Edition
Debbie & Richard Lawrence

God's Design® for Heaven & Earth
Our Weather & Water Teacher Supplement

Reprinted September 2018

Fourth edition. Copyright © 2008, 2016 by Debbie & Richard Lawrence.

ISBN: 978-1-62691-450-6

Published by Answers in Genesis, PO Box 510, Hebron, KY 41048

Book designer: Diane King
Editor: Gary Vaterlaus

The publisher and authors have made every reasonable effort to ensure that the activities recommended in this book are safe when performed as instructed but assume no responsibility for any damage caused or sustained while conducting the experiments and activities. It is the parents', guardians', and/or teachers' responsibility to supervise all recommended activities.

Printed in China.

AnswersInGenesis.org • GodsDesign.com

Welcome to GOD'S DESIGN®

HEAVEN & EARTH

God's Design for Heaven and Earth is a series that has been designed for use in teaching earth science to elementary and middle school students. It is divided into three books: *Our Universe*, *Our Planet Earth*, and *Our Weather and Water*. Each book has 35 lessons including a final project that ties all of the lessons together.

In addition to the lessons, special features in each book include biographical information on interesting people as well as fun facts to make the subject more fun.

Although this is a complete curriculum, the information included here is just a beginning, so please feel free to add to each lesson as you see fit. A resource guide is included in the appendices to help you find additional information and resources. A list of supplies needed is included at the beginning of each lesson, while a master list of all supplies needed for the entire series can be found in the appendices.

Answer keys for all review questions, worksheets, quizzes, and the final exam are included here. Reproducible student worksheets and tests may be found in the digital download that comes with the purchase of the curriculum. You may download these files from GodsDesign.com/HeavenEarth.

If you prefer the files on a CD-ROM, you can order that from Answers in Genesis at an additional cost by calling 800-778-3390.

If you wish to get through all three books of the *Heaven and Earth* series in one year, plan on covering approximately three lessons per week. The time required for each lesson varies depending on how much additional information you include, but plan on 40 to 45 minutes for grades 3–8.

Quizzes may be given at the conclusion of each unit and the final exam may be given after lesson 34.

If you wish to cover the material in more depth, you may add additional information and take a longer period of time to cover all the material, or you could choose to do only one or two of the books in the series as a unit study.

Why Teach Earth Science?

It is not uncommon to question the need to teach children hands-on science in elementary or middle school. We could argue that the knowledge gained in science will be needed later in life in order for children to be more productive and well-rounded adults. We could argue that teaching children science also teaches them logical and inductive thinking and reasoning skills, which are tools they will need to be more successful. We could argue that science is a necessity in this technological world in which we live. While all of these arguments are true, not one of them is the main reason that we should teach our children science. The most important reason to teach science in elementary school is to give children an understanding that God is our Creator, and the Bible can be trusted. Teaching science from a creation perspective is one of the best ways to reinforce our children's faith in God and to help them counter the evolutionary propaganda they face every day.

God is the Master Creator of everything. His handiwork is all around us. Our great Creator put in place all of the laws of physics, biology, and chemistry. These laws were put here for us to see His wisdom and power. In science, we see the hand of God at work more than in any other subject. Romans 1:20 says, "For since the creation of the world His invisible attributes are clearly seen, being understood by the things that are made, even His eternal power and Godhead, so that they [men] are without excuse." We need to help our children see God as Creator of the world around them so they will be able to recognize God and follow Him.

The study of earth science helps us to understand and appreciate this amazing world God gave us. Studying the processes that shape the earth, and exploring the origins of the earth and the universe often bring us into direct conflict with evolutionary theories. This is why it is so critical to teach our children the truth of the Bible, how to evaluate the evidence, how to distinguish fact from theory, and to realize that the evidence, rightly interpreted, supports biblical creation not evolution.

It's fun to teach earth science! It's interesting too. Rocks, weather, and stars are all around us. Children naturally collect rocks and gaze at the stars. You just need to direct their curiosity.

Finally, teaching earth science is easy. It's where you live. You won't have to try to find strange materials for experiments or do dangerous things to learn about the earth.

How Do I Teach Science?

In order to teach any subject you need to understand how people learn. People learn in different ways. Most people, and children in particular, have a dominant or preferred learning style in which they absorb and retain information more easily.

If a student's dominant style is:

Auditory
He needs not only to hear the information but he needs to hear himself say it. This child needs oral presentation as well as oral drill and repetition.

Visual
She needs things she can see. This child responds well to flashcards, pictures, charts, models, etc.

Kinesthetic
He needs active participation. This child remembers best through games, hands-on activities, experiments, and field trips.

Also, some people are more relational while others are more analytical. The relational student needs to know why this subject is important, and how it will affect him personally. The analytical student, however, wants just the facts.

If you are trying to teach more than one student, you will probably have to deal with more than one learning style. Therefore, you need to present your lessons in several different ways so that each student can grasp and retain the information.

Grades 3–8
The first part of each lesson should be completed by all upper elementary and junior high students. This is the main part of the lesson containing a reading section, a hands-on activity that reinforces the ideas in the reading section (blue box), and a review section that provides review questions and application questions.

Grades 6–8
In addition, for middle school/junior high age students, we provide a "Challenge" section that contains more challenging material as well as additional activities and projects for older students (green box).

We have included periodic biographies to help your students appreciate the great men and women who have gone before us in the field of science.

We suggest a threefold approach to each lesson:

Introduce the topic

We give a brief description of the facts. Frequently you will want to add more information than the essentials given in this book. In addition to reading this section aloud (or having older children read it on their own), you may wish to do one or more of the following:

- Read a related book with your students.
- Write things down to help your visual learners.
- Give some history of the subject. We provide some historical sketches to help you, but you may want to add more.
- Ask questions to get your students thinking about the subject.

Make observations and do experiments

- Hands-on projects are suggested for each lesson. This part of each lesson may require help from the teacher.
- Have your students perform the activity by themselves whenever possible.

Review

- The "What did we learn?" section has review questions.
- The "Taking it further" section encourages students to
  - Draw conclusions
  - Make applications of what was learned
  - Add extended information to what was covered in the lesson
- The "FUN FACT" section adds fun or interesting information.

By teaching all three parts of the lesson, you will be presenting the material in a way that children with any learning style can both relate to and remember.

Also, this approach relates directly to the scientific method and will help your students think more scientifically. The *scientific method* is just a way to examine a subject logically and learn from it. Briefly, the steps of the scientific method are:

1. Learn about a topic.
2. Ask a question.
3. Make a hypothesis (a good guess).
4. Design an experiment to test your hypothesis.
5. Observe the experiment and collect data.
6. Draw conclusions. (Does the data support your hypothesis?)

Note: It's okay to have a "wrong hypothesis." That's how we learn. Be sure to help your students understand why they sometimes get a different result than expected.

Our lessons will help your students begin to approach problems in a logical, scientific way.

How Do I Teach Creation vs. Evolution?

We are constantly bombarded by evolutionary ideas about the earth in books, movies, museums, and even commercials. These raise many questions: What is the big bang? How old is the earth? Do fossils show evolution to be true? Was there really a worldwide flood? When did dinosaurs live? Was there an ice age? How can we teach our children the truth about the origins of the earth? The Bible answers these questions and this book accepts the historical accuracy of the Bible as written. We believe this is the only way we can teach our children to trust that everything God says is true.

There are five common views of the origins of life and the age of the earth:

Historical biblical account	Progressive creation	Gap theory	Theistic evolution	Naturalistic evolution
Each day of creation in Genesis is a normal day of about 24 hours in length, in which God created everything that exists. The earth is only thousands of years old, as determined by the genealogies in the Bible.	The idea that God created various creatures to replace other creatures that died out over millions of years. Each of the days in Genesis represents a long period of time (day-age view) and the earth is billions of years old.	The idea that there was a long, long time between what happened in Genesis 1:1 and what happened in Genesis 1:2. During this time, the "fossil record" was supposed to have formed, and millions of years of earth history supposedly passed.	The idea that God used the process of evolution over millions of years (involving struggle and death) to bring about what we see today.	The view that there is no God and evolution of all life forms happened by purely naturalistic processes over billions of years.

Any theory that tries to combine the evolutionary time frame with creation presupposes that death entered the world before Adam sinned, which contradicts what God has said in His Word. The view that the earth (and its "fossil record") is hundreds of millions of years old damages the gospel message. God's completed creation was "very good" at the end of the sixth day (Genesis 1:31). Death entered this perfect paradise *after* Adam disobeyed God's command. It was the punishment for Adam's sin (Genesis 2:16–17, 3:19; Romans 5:12–19). Thorns appeared when God cursed the ground because of Adam's sin (Genesis 3:18).

The first animal death occurred when God killed at least one animal, shedding its blood, to make clothes for Adam and Eve (Genesis 3:21). If the earth's "fossil record" (filled with death, disease, and thorns) formed over millions of years before Adam appeared (and before he sinned), then death no longer would be the penalty for sin. Death, the "last enemy" (1 Corinthians 15:26), diseases (such as cancer), and thorns would instead be part of the original creation that God labeled "very good." No, it is clear that the "fossil record" formed some time *after* Adam sinned—not many millions of years before. Most fossils were formed as a result of the worldwide Genesis Flood.

When viewed from a biblical perspective, the scientific evidence clearly supports a recent creation by God, and not naturalistic evolution and millions of years. The volume of evidence supporting the biblical creation account is substantial and cannot be adequately covered in this book. If you would like more information on this topic, please see the resource guide in Appendix A. To help get you started, just a few examples of evidence supporting biblical creation are given below:

Evolutionary Myth: The earth is 4.6 billion years old.

The Truth: Many processes observed today point to a young earth of only a few thousand years. The rate at which the earth's magnetic field is decaying suggests the earth must be less than 10,000 years old. The rate of population growth and the recent emergence of civilization suggests only a few thousand years of human population. And, at the current rate of accumulation, the amount of mud on the sea floor should be many kilometers thick if the earth were billions of years old. However, the average depth of all the mud in the whole ocean is less than 400 meters, giving a maximum age for the earth of not more than 12 million years. All this and more indicates an earth much younger than 4.6 billion years.

John D. Morris, *The Young Earth* (Creation Life Publishers, 1994), pp. 70–71, 83–90. See also "Get Answers: Young Age Evidence" at www.answersingenesis.org/go/young.

Evolutionary Myth: The universe formed from the big bang.

The Truth: There are many problems with this theory. It does not explain where the initial material came from. It cannot explain what caused that material to fly apart in the first place. And nothing in physics indicates what would make the particles begin to stick together instead of flying off into space forever. The big bang theory contradicts many scientific laws. Because of these problems, some scientists have abandoned the big bang and are attempting to develop new theories to explain the origin of the universe.

Jason Lisle, "Does the Big Bang Fit with the Bible," in *The New Answers Book 2*, Ken Ham, ed. (Master Books, 2008). See also "What are some of the problems with the big bang hypothesis?" at www.answersingenesis.org/go/big-bang.

Evolutionary Myth: Fossils prove evolution.

The Truth: While Darwin predicted that the fossil record would show numerous transitional fossils, even more than 145 years later, all we have are a handful of disputable examples. For example, there are no fossils showing something that is part way between a dinosaur and a bird. Fossils show that a snail has always been a snail; a squid has always been a squid. God created each animal to reproduce after its kind (Genesis 1:20–25).

Evolutionary Myth: There is not enough water for a worldwide flood.

The Truth: Prior to the Flood, just as today, much of the water was stored beneath the surface of the earth. In addition, Genesis 1 states that the water below was separated from the water above, indicating that the atmosphere may have contained a great deal more water than it does today. Also, it is likely that before the Flood the mountains were not as high as they are today, but that the mountains rose and the valleys sank *after* the Flood began, as Psalm 104:6–9 suggests. At the beginning of the Flood, the fountains of the deep burst forth and it rained for 40 days and nights. This could have provided more than enough water to flood the entire earth. Indeed, if the entire earth's surface were leveled by smoothing out the topography of not only the land surface but also the rock surface on the ocean floor, the waters of the present-day oceans would cover the earth's surface to a depth of 1.7 miles (2.7 kilometers). Fossils have been found on the highest mountain peaks around the world showing that the waters of the Flood did indeed cover the entire earth.

Ken Ham & Tim Lovett, "What There Really a Noah's Ark and Flood," in *The New Answers Book 1*, Ken Ham, ed. (Master Books, 2006).

Evolutionary Myth: Slow climate changes over time have resulted in multiple ice ages.

The Truth: There is widespread evidence of glaciers in many parts of the world indicating one ice age. Evolutionists find the cause of the Ice Age a mystery. Obviously, the climate would need to be colder. But global cooling by itself is not enough, because then there would be less evaporation, so less snow. How is it possible to have both a cold climate and lots of evaporation? The Ice Age was most likely an aftermath of Noah's Flood. When "all the fountains of the great deep" broke up, much hot water and lava would have poured directly into the oceans. This would have warmed the oceans, increasing evaporation. At the same time, much volcanic ash in the air after the Flood would have blocked out much sunlight, cooling the land. So the Flood would have produced the necessary combination of increased evaporation from the warmed oceans and cool continental climate from the volcanic ash in the air. This would have resulted in increased snowfall over the continents. With the snow falling faster than it melted, ice sheets would have built up. The Ice Age probably lasted less than 700 years.

Michael Oard, *Frozen in Time* (Master Books, 2004). See also www.answersingenesis.org/go/ice-age.

Evolutionary Myth: Thousands of random changes over millions of years resulted in the earth we see today.

The Truth: The second law of thermodynamics describes how any system tends toward a state of zero entropy or disorder. We observe how everything around us becomes less organized and loses energy. The changes required for the formation of the universe, the planet earth and life, all from disorder, run counter to the physical laws we see at work today. There is no known mechanism to harness the raw energy of the universe and generate the specified complexity we see all around us.

John D. Morris, *The Young Earth* (Creation Life Publishers, 1994), p. 43. See also www.answersingenesis.org/go/thermodynamics.

Despite the claims of many scientists, if you examine the evidence objectively, it is obvious that evolution and millions of years have not been proven. You can be confident that if you teach that what the Bible says is true, you won't go wrong. Instill in your student a confidence in the truth of the Bible in all areas. If scientific thought seems to contradict the Bible, realize that scientists often make mistakes, but God does not lie. At one time scientists believed that the earth was the center of the universe, that living things could spring from non-living things, and that blood-letting was good for the body. All of these were believed to be scientific facts but have since been disproved, but the Word of God remains true. If we use modern "science" to interpret the Bible, what will happen to our faith in God's Word when scientists change their theories yet again?

Integrating the Seven C's

The Seven C's is a framework in which all of history, and the future to come, can be placed. As we go through our daily routines we may not understand how the details of life connect with the truth that we find in the Bible. This is also the case for students. When discussing the importance of the Bible you may find yourself telling students that the Bible is relevant in everyday activities. But how do we help the younger generation see that? The Seven C's are intended to help.

The Seven C's can be used to develop a biblical worldview in students, young or old. Much more than entertaining stories and religious teachings, the Bible has real connections to our everyday life. It may be hard, at first, to see how many connections there are, but with practice, the daily relevance of God's Word will come alive. Let's look at the Seven C's of History and how each can be connected to what the students are learning.

Creation

God perfectly created the heavens, the earth, and all that is in them in six normal-length days around 6,000 years ago.

This teaching is foundational to a biblical worldview and can be put into the context of any subject. In science, the amazing design that we see in nature—whether in the veins of a leaf or the complexity of your hand—is all the handiwork of God. Virtually all of the lessons in *God's Design for Science* can be related to God's creation of the heavens and earth.

Other contexts include:

Natural laws—any discussion of a law of nature naturally leads to God's creative power.

DNA and information—the information in every living thing was created by God's supreme intelligence.

Mathematics—the laws of mathematics reflect the order of the Creator.

Biological diversity—the distinct kinds of animals that we see were created during the Creation Week, not as products of evolution.

Art—the creativity of man is demonstrated through various art forms.

History—all time scales can be compared to the biblical time scale extending back about 6,000 years.

Ecology—God has called mankind to act as stewards over His creation.

Corruption

After God completed His perfect creation, Adam disobeyed God by eating the forbidden fruit. As a result, sin and death entered the world, and the world has been in decay since that time. This point is evident throughout the world that we live in. The struggle for survival in animals, the death of loved ones, and the violence all around us are all examples of the corrupting influence of sin.

Other contexts include:

Genetics—the mutations that lead to diseases, cancer, and variation within populations are the result of corruption.

Biological relationships—predators and parasites result from corruption.

History—wars and struggles between mankind, exemplified in the account of Cain and Abel, are a result of sin.

Catastrophe

God was grieved by the wickedness of mankind and judged this wickedness with a global Flood. The Flood covered the entire surface of the earth and killed all air-breathing creatures that were not aboard the Ark. The eight people and the animals aboard the Ark replenished the earth after God delivered them from the catastrophe.

The catastrophe described in the Bible would naturally leave behind much evidence. The studies of geology and of the biological diversity of animals on the planet are two of the most obvious applications of this event. Much of scientific understanding is based on how a scientist views the events of the Genesis Flood.

Other contexts include:

Biological diversity—all of the birds, mammals, and other air-breathing animals have populated the earth from the original kinds which left the Ark.

Geology—the layers of sedimentary rock seen in road-cuts, canyons, and other geologic features are testaments to the global Flood.

Geography—features like mountains, valleys, and plains were formed as the floodwaters receded.

Physics—rainbows are a perennial sign of God's faithfulness and His pledge to never flood the entire earth again.

Fossils—Most fossils are a result of the Flood rapidly burying plants and animals.

Plate tectonics—the rapid movement of the earth's plates likely accompanied the Flood.

Global warming/Ice Age—both of these items are likely a result of the activity of the Flood. The warming we are experiencing today has been present since the peak of the Ice Age (with variations over time).

Confusion

God commanded Noah and his descendants to spread across the earth. The refusal to obey this command and the building of the tower at Babel caused God to judge this sin. The common language of the people was confused and they spread across the globe as groups with a common language. All people are truly of "one blood" as descendants of Noah and, originally, Adam.

The confusion of the languages led people to scatter across the globe. As people settled in new areas, the traits they carried with them became concentrated in those populations. Traits like dark skin were beneficial in the tropics while other traits benefited populations in northern climates, and distinct people groups, not races, developed.

Other contexts include:

Genetics—the study of human DNA has shown that there is little difference in the genetic makeup of the so-called "races."

Languages—there are about seventy language groups from which all modern languages have developed.

Archaeology—the presence of common building structures, like pyramids, around the world confirms the biblical account.

Literature—recorded and oral records tell of similar events relating to the Flood and the dispersion at Babel.

Christ

God did not leave mankind without a way to be redeemed from its sinful state. The Law was given to Moses to show how far away man is from God's standard of perfection. Rather than the sacrifices, which only covered sins, people needed a Savior to take away their sin. This was accomplished when Jesus Christ came to earth to live a perfect life and, by that obedience, was able to be the sacrifice to satisfy God's wrath for all who believe.

The deity of Christ and the amazing plan that was set forth before the foundation of the earth is the core of Christian doctrine. The earthly life of Jesus was the fulfillment of many prophecies and confirms the truthfulness of the Bible. His miracles and presence in human form demonstrate that God is both intimately concerned with His creation and able to control it in an absolute way.

Other contexts include:

Psychology—popular secular psychology teaches of the inherent goodness of man, but Christ has lived the only perfect life. Mankind needs a Savior to redeem it from its unrighteousness.

Biology—Christ's virgin birth demonstrates God's sovereignty over nature.

Physics—turning the water into wine and the feeding of the five thousand demonstrate Christ's deity and His sovereignty over nature.

History—time is marked (in the western world) based on the birth of Christ despite current efforts to change the meaning.

Art—much art is based on the life of Christ and many of the masters are known for these depictions, whether on canvas or in music.

Cross

Because God is perfectly just and holy, He must punish sin. The sinless life of Jesus Christ was offered as a substitutionary sacrifice for all of those who will repent and put their faith in the Savior. After His death on the Cross, He defeated death by rising on the third day and is now seated at the right hand of God.

The events surrounding the crucifixion and resurrection have a most significant place in the life of Christians.

Though there is no way to scientifically prove the resurrection, there is likewise no way to prove the stories of evolutionary history. These are matters of faith founded in the truth of God's Word and His character. The eyewitness testimony of over 500 people and the written Word of God provide the basis for our belief.

Other contexts include:

Biology—the biological details of the crucifixion can be studied alongside the anatomy of the human body.

History—the use of crucifixion as a method of punishment was short-lived in historical terms and not known at the time it was prophesied.

Art—the crucifixion and resurrection have inspired many wonderful works of art.

Consummation

God, in His great mercy, has promised that He will restore the earth to its original state—a world without death, suffering, war, and disease. The corruption introduced by Adam's sin will be removed. Those who have repented and put their trust in the completed work of Christ on the Cross will experience life in this new heaven and earth. We will be able to enjoy and worship God forever in a perfect place.

This future event is a little more difficult to connect with academic subjects. However, the hope of a life in God's presence and in the absence of sin can be inserted in discussions of human conflict, disease, suffering, and sin in general.

Other contexts include:

History—in discussions of war or human conflict the coming age offers hope.

Biology—the violent struggle for life seen in the predator-prey relationships will no longer taint the earth.

Medicine—while we struggle to find cures for diseases and alleviate the suffering of those enduring the effects of the Curse, we ultimately place our hope in the healing that will come in the eternal state.

The preceding examples are given to provide ideas for integrating the Seven C's of History into a broad range of curriculum activities. We would recommend that you give your students, and yourself, a better understanding of the Seven C's framework by using AiG's *Answers for Kids* curriculum. The first seven lessons of this curriculum cover the Seven C's and will establish a solid understanding of the true history, and future, of the universe. Full lesson plans, activities, and student resources are provided in the curriculum set.

We also offer bookmarks displaying the Seven C's and a wall chart. These can be used as visual cues for the students to help them recall the information and integrate new learning into its proper place in a biblical worldview.

Even if you use other curricula, you can still incorporate the Seven C's teaching into those. Using this approach will help students make firm connections between biblical events and every aspect of the world around them, and they will begin to develop a truly biblical worldview and not just add pieces of the Bible to what they learn in "the real world."

Atmosphere & Meteorology

1 A Christian View of Weather

What does the Bible say?

Supply list

Copy of "Weather Across the Country" worksheet
Newspaper weather report

Supplies for Challenge

Research materials on various Christian scientists

What did we learn?

- Is there a Christian view of weather? **Yes, there is a Christian view of everything. Either the weather is only naturalistic, or it is a result of a system designed by God the Creator.**

- What three events described in the Bible have greatly affected the weather on earth? **Creation, the Curse due to the Fall of man, and the Flood.**

- List three things you can learn about the weather from a newspaper weather report. **Actual high and low temperatures, predicted high and low temperatures, precipitation amounts, weather front locations, record high and low temperatures, weather conditions across the country.**

Taking it further

- Why is it important to have a Christian view of weather? **It allows us to recognize God's handiwork.**

- What are some geographical or physical characteristics that affect the weather in a particular area? **Large bodies of water, mountains, deserts, latitude, altitude.**

2 Structure of the Atmosphere

Layers above the earth

Supply list

Candle	Matches
Glass jar	Dish
Modeling clay	

Supplies for Challenge

Graph paper

What did we learn?

- What are the two main components of air? **Nitrogen—78%, Oxygen—21%.**

- What are the five levels of the atmosphere? **Troposphere, stratosphere, mesosphere, thermosphere, exosphere. The lesson also mentioned the ionosphere and magnetosphere.**

- What are some ways that the atmosphere protects us? **It protects us from extreme temperatures, vacuums, solar radiation and meteors, and provides oxygen to breathe.**

Taking it further

- How would the earth be different if there were a higher concentration of oxygen? **Fires would burn uncontrollably.**
- What would happen if the nitrogen in the atmosphere was replaced with a more reactive element, such as carbon? **The carbon would combine with the oxygen and form carbon dioxide, making the air unbreathable.**

Challenge: Atmospheric Temperature

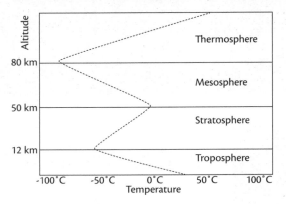

3 The Weight of Air

It has weight?

Supply list

Yard or meter stick	Tape
2 identical balloons	String

Supplies for Challenge

Wide mouth jar	String or rubberband
Plastic grocery bag	

What did we learn

- What causes air to have weight? **Gravity pulling down on the air molecules.**
- How much air pressure do we experience at sea level? **About 15 pounds per square inch.**
- Why don't we feel the weight of the air molecules? **Our bodies push out with the same amount of pressure.**

- Do you expect air pressure to be the same at all locations in the world? **No, as you go up in altitude, gravity exerts less force on the air molecules so there is less air pressure. Also, the pressure varies from one area to another causing weather fronts.**

Taking it further

- Why is it important that air has weight? **The weight of the air allows us to have wind and moving air fronts.**
- Why must aircraft be pressurized when flying at high altitudes? **The air pressure is much lower at high altitudes than it is on the ground and the lack of pressure can be painful for passengers, especially on their ears as they try to adjust to the lower pressure. If the pressure is low enough, there might not be enough oxygen to breathe.**

4 The Study of Weather

An introduction to meteorology

Supply list

Baking dish (white or light color works best)	
Styrofoam cups	Ice
Food coloring	Boiling water

Supplies for Challenge

Copy of "Weather Ingredients" worksheet

What did we learn?

- What is meteorology? **The study of the atmosphere; particularly the study of the conditions of the troposphere.**
- What are the five important conditions in the troposphere that meteorologists study? **Temperature, atmospheric/air pressure, humidity, wind, and precipitation.**

Taking it further

- Why are meteorologists interested in studying the conditions of the troposphere? **They want to understand what affects the weather and be able to predict future weather conditions.**
- How does the sun heat areas of the earth that do not receive much direct sunlight? **The sunlight is most concentrated in areas close to the equator. The air is warmer there than at the poles. However, because of air and water currents, warmer air and warmer water move toward the poles and cooler air and water move toward the equator so the earth is more evenly heated.**

Challenge: Weather Ingredients worksheet

	Earth	Sun	Air	Water
W	Winter	Waves	Warm/Wind	Wet/White caps
E	Elevation	Eclipse	Expands	Evaporation
A	Absorbs	Angle	Atmosphere	Acid rain
T	Tilted axis	Temperature	Troposphere	Thunderstorm
H	Huge	Heat	Humidity	Hail/Humidity
E	Equator	Energy	Electricity	El Niño/Eye of storm
R	Rotation/Revolution	Radiation/Reflect	Relative humidity	Rain

QUIZ 1

Atmosphere & Meteorology

Lessons 1–4

Short answer:

1. What does it mean to have a Christian view of weather? **It means to recognize that God designed weather to work the way it does and He controls it. Everything is not just random chance.**

2. Name three things you might find in a local weather report. **Forecasted temperatures and precipitation, actual temperatures and precipitation, location of weather fronts, record temperatures, weather across the country.**

3. What is the outermost part of the atmosphere called? **The exosphere.**

4. What three events recorded in the Bible drastically affected the surface of the earth? **Creation, Fall, and Flood.**

5. What two gases comprise the majority of our atmosphere? **Nitrogen and oxygen.**

6. List three ways the atmosphere protects life on earth. **Protects us from the vacuum of space, protects from harmful radiation, protects from extreme temperatures, provides air to breathe.**

7. What are scientists called who study the atmosphere? **meteorologists.**

8. What is temperature? **Measurement of the energy in the atmosphere.**

9. What causes air pressure? **Gravity pulling down on air molecules.**

10. What is absolute humidity? **The total amount of moisture in the air.**

11. What is relative humidity? **The ratio of the amount of moisture in the air to the total amount of moisture the air could hold at the current temperature.**

12. What is precipitation? **Moisture that falls from the atmosphere.**

13. What is the major cause of wind? **Heating of the air by the sun's rays.**

14. Weather occurs in which part of the atmosphere? **Troposphere.**

15. What happens to the atmospheric pressure as you go up in altitude? **The pressure goes down.**

Challenge questions

Short answer:

16. Name at least two Christian scientists from the past. **Sir Isaac Newton, Lord Kelvin, Blaise Pascal, Johannes Kepler, Carl Linneaus, Robert Boyle, Charles Babbage, Joseph Lister, Georges Cuvier, David Brewster, Louis Pasteur, James Clerk Maxwell.**

17. What is lapse rate with respect to the atmosphere? **The rate at which the temperature decreases as you increase in altitude.**

18. Name two gases that are lighter than air. **Hydrogen and helium.**

19. Briefly explain how each of the following contributes to weather formation.

Sun: **Generates energy waves that heat up the earth.**

Earth: **Absorbs heat from the sun and radiates it into the atmosphere.**

Air: **Absorbs heat from the sun and the earth causing molecules to move around and changes air pressure creating wind and weather fronts.**

Water: **Evaporation and condensation of water contributes to much of the weather we experience.**

20. Does temperature always decrease with altitude? Explain your answer. **No. Above the troposphere temperatures increase with altitude through the stratosphere, decrease with altitude in the mesosphere, and increase with altitude in the thermosphere.**

Ancient Weather & Climate

5 Weather vs. Climate

What's the difference?

Supply list

Copy of "Weather vs. Climate" worksheet

Newspaper weather report   World atlas

Supplies for Challenge

Copy of "World Map"   World atlas

Colored pencils

What did we learn?

- What is weather? **The atmospheric conditions present in an area at a given time.**

- What is climate? **The average weather conditions for an area over a long period of time, including average temperatures and average precipitation.**

- What are the five major climates found on earth? **Polar, desert, tropical, subtropical, and temperate.**

Taking it further

- How does the Gobi Desert help create the monsoon? **The Gobi Desert heats the dry air around it. That air rises, allowing cooler air to move in. The cooler air comes from the Bay of Bengal and has a high moisture content, thus bringing rain to the area near the bay.**

- Which of the following phrases describe weather and which describe climate?

  Cloudy with a chance of rain: **Weather.**

  Average of 20 inches of rain per year: **Climate.**

  Average summer temperature of 70°F: **Climate.**

  3 inches of snow in the past 24 hours: **Weather.**

6 Pre-Flood Climate

Was it different?

Supply list

Mirror   Plate or shallow dish

House plant

Supplies for Challenge

Copy of "Climate Clues" worksheet

What did we learn?

- Using clues from the Bible and science, what was the climate most likely like on earth before the

Flood? **Warm; possibly no rain and more water vapor in the atmosphere; more constant temperature.**

Taking it further

- How does the Bible say that plants were watered in the beginning? **The Bible says they were watered by springs and rivers. They were also probably watered by dew and from underground sources.**

- How might the breaking up of the original landmass have contributed to the Flood? **Superheated water from inside the earth would have shot into the atmosphere and then rained back to earth.**

Challenge: Climate Clues worksheet

Clue #1:

1. Where do swamp cypress trees grow today? **Swampy areas in Georgia and Florida.**

2. What is the climate like in the Arctic Islands today? **Very cold and snowy.**

3. What possible explanation could there be for how the cypress tree fossils were formed in the Arctic Islands? **It may have been much warmer and wetter in the past so the trees could grow there, or the cypress trees were carried there from another location and then fossilized.**

Clue #2:

1. Where do hippopotami live today? **In grasslands where there is still water or in forests in Africa.**

2. What kind of plant life is required to support elephants? **An elephant eats 200–400 pounds of grass and other plants each day.**

3. Do many people live in villages in the Sahara Desert today? **Although there are some villages, most people that live in the desert are nomads.**

4. What can you conclude about the climate in the Sahara area before the Flood? **There must have been a lot more water and grass to support the life that was there.**

Clue #3:

1. What is the climate like in Antarctica today? **It is very cold and snowy—mostly frozen.**

2. What kind of plant life is required to support dinosaurs? **It depends what kind of dinosaurs they were; they either ate plants or they ate the animals that ate the plants.**

3. What kind of plant life exists in Antarctica today? **There is very little plant life there.**

4. What can you conclude about the climate in Antarctica before the Flood? **It was probably much warmer than it is now.**

7 Climate Changes Due to the Genesis Flood

God's punishment for sin

Supply list

Paper
Drawing materials (colored pencils, markers, etc.)

What did we learn?

- What was the earth's climate like before the Flood? **Probably more uniformly warm and tropical.**

- What was the climate like after the Flood? **It was much cooler and wetter than today. Ice covered much of the earth. It was still temperate in the areas near the equator.**

- Approximately how much of the world was covered with ice during the Ice Age? **30%.**

- What two weather conditions are necessary for an ice age to form? **Cool summers and wet/snowy winters.**

Taking it further

- Why did God send a huge Flood? **To destroy man because of his wickedness.**

- What evidence points to a warmer pre-Flood climate? **Fossils of tropical plants around the world.**

- What evidence points to an ice age? **Valleys cut by glaciers, frozen plants and animals, fossils in ice, etc.**

- Do we see new glaciers forming today? **Yes, we see some new glaciers forming and some old glaciers growing bigger for a few years, but not on the large scale that occurred during the Ice Age.**

8 Global Warming

Fact or Fiction

Supply list

Articles about global warming or climate change

What did we learn?

- What is global warming? **The increase in average temperature around the earth.**
- What is the greenhouse effect? **Heat is trapped in the atmosphere and not released back into space.**
- What is the main cause of the greenhouse effect? **Water vapor in the atmosphere.**
- What amount of greenhouse effect is due to carbon dioxide in the atmosphere? **Only about 5%.**
- How much has the temperature increased over the past 130 years? **Only about 1.2°F.**

- Name at least two possible natural causes for increased temperatures. **Increased energy from the sun, decreased volcanic activity, increased cloud cover.**

Taking it further

- Why is it important to know what assumptions are made when looking at computer models? **The assumptions greatly affect the outcome. If bad assumptions are made, then the results are unreliable.**
- Ice core samples from Greenland indicate that rapid climate shifts have occurred in the past. How can your worldview affect the interpretation of this data? **If you believe the Bible you would expect to see rapid climate changes due to the Flood and its aftermath. If you believe in evolutionary processes and slow changes, this data can be very alarming and cause people to look for possible rapid climate changes in the future.**

QUIZ 2 Ancient Weather & Climate

Lessons 5–8

Match the term with its definition.

1. _F_ Conditions in the atmosphere at a given time
2. _C_ Average weather conditions over a long time
3. _I_ Very dry climate
4. _A_ Wet warm climate year round
5. _H_ How plants were watered in the beginning
6. _B_ Event believed to be triggered by the Flood
7. _D_ Trapping of heat in the earth's atmosphere
8. _E_ Increase in Earth's average temperature due to increased carbon dioxide
9. _J_ Climate with four distinct seasons
10. _G_ Climate with cooler winters than tropical areas

Mark each statement as either True or False.

11. _T_ Average global temperatures have increased in the past 150 years.

12. _F_ Carbon dioxide is the main cause of the greenhouse effect.
13. _F_ It has been proven that global warming is caused by man's actions.
14. _T_ The earth's climate was probably more uniformly tropical before the Flood.
15. _F_ The Flood did not change the earth very much.
16. _T_ The Bible indicates there may have been one landmass before the Flood.
17. _F_ The climate changes from day to day.
18. _T_ Deserts can be cold.
19. _T_ The monsoon brings rain to much of Southeast Asia.
20. _F_ We should just ignore global warming.

Challenge questions

Short answer:

21. Describe the Coriolis effect. **Circular air currents develop due to the rotation of the earth—primarily counter clockwise in the northern hemisphere and clockwise in the southern hemisphere.**

22. In an area that primarily experiences updrafts, would you expect the weather to be wet or dry? Why would you expect this? **Rising air increases precipitation so it would be wet.**

23. Explain how finding fossils of dinosaurs in Antarctica gives a clue to its past climate. **In order for dinosaurs to exist they need plants or other animals to eat, so the climate had to have been warm enough to support this kind of life.**

24. How could the climate in an area have changed quickly in the past? **The Genesis Flood caused many changes to the earth, which greatly affected the climate in a short period of time. In general, rapid climate changes do not occur; the Flood was a very unusual event.**

25. Give an example of how global warming could be a beneficial thing. **Longer growing seasons, increased precipitation, fewer deaths due to the cold, increased shipping in northern areas.**

Unit 3
Clouds

9 Water Cycle

The ultimate in recycling

Supply list

Paper   Colored pencils

What did we learn?

- How does water vapor enter the atmosphere? **Through evaporation, transpiration, and vaporization.**
- Which of these processes accounts for most of the water in the air? **Evaporation.**
- How does water get from the atmosphere back to the earth? **Through precipitation such as rain, snow, sleet, dew, and hail.**

Taking it further

- What are some factors that affect how fast the water evaporates from the surface of the ocean or lake? **Wind, heat, and the dryness of the air all affect the rate of evaporation.**
- Why is it better to water your grass early in the morning rather than later in the day during the summer? **The air is hotter in the middle of the day and more of the water will evaporate and less will soak into the ground to help the grass grow.**

10 Cloud Formation

Pretty white shapes in the sky

Supply list

Pan of water   Plastic zipper bag
Jar with a lid   Ice

Supplies for Challenge:

Black construction paper   Hammer
Gloves   Flashlight
Newspaper   Towel
2 shoe boxes (one must be smaller than the other)
Lid or cardboard for smaller shoe box
Several small pieces of dry ice

What did we learn?

- What is a cloud? **A mass of water droplets or ice crystals suspended in the air.**
- What is the dew point of air? **The point at which the air is holding the maximum amount of water for the current temperature.**
- What is another name for dew point? **100% relative humidity.**
- How do clouds form? **Warm moist air rises. As it rises, it cools. Eventually it reaches the dew point and water condenses on dust and pollen particles to form clouds.**

Taking it further

- Often, one side of a mountain range receives much more rain than the other side. Why do you think this happens? **If the winds come primarily from one direction, clouds will form more often on the near side of the mountain. As these clouds are forced to rise, they cool and can no longer hold all of the water, resulting in precipitation on that side of the mountain.**

- Why don't clouds always result in rain? **If the air around a cloud is dry, the water in the cloud will evaporate again instead of raining.**

- What role do pollen and dust play in cloud formation? **Water at dew point needs something on which to condense. Dust and pollen particles in the air provide this and thus encourage condensation and cloud formation.**

Cloud Types

A beautiful variety

Supply list

Blue construction paper   Cotton balls
Glue

Supplies for Challenge

Clear 2-liter plastic bottle   Match
Warm water

What did we learn?

- What are the two ways that clouds are classified? **By shape and altitude.**

- What are the three main shapes of clouds and how does each look? **Stratus—stretched out layers; cumulus—heaped, piled up, and fluffy; cirrus—curly or wispy.**
- What are rain clouds called? **Nimbus clouds.**

Taking it further

- What would a fluffy cloud at 0.5 miles (0.8 km) be called? **Stratocumulus.**
- What would a wispy cloud at 5 miles (8 km) above the earth be called? **Cirrus—it would be cirrus by shape and cirrus by altitude but would not be called cirrocirrus, just cirrus.**

Precipitation

Rain, rain go away

Supply list

Flour   Rain/water
Pie pan/baking dish   Access to oven

Supplies for Challenge

pH testing paper (optional)
Samples of water from various locations near your home

What did we learn?

- What are the main types of precipitation? **Dew, frost, drizzle, rain, sleet, hail, and snow.**

- What is the difference between drizzle and rain? **Drizzle is very tiny drops; rain is water droplets larger than 0.02 inches (0.05 cm).**
- What shape do snowflakes have? **Each is unique but they all have six sides—hexagonal.**
- What is coalescence? **When water droplets begin to stick together to form bigger drops.**
- What is the difference between sleet and hail? **Sleet is very small ice pellets, while hail is larger pellets of ice.**

Taking it further

- What conditions are necessary for large hailstones to form? **Warm humid conditions are needed to form** the strong updrafts necessary to keep the ice pellets in the air long enough to become hail.

- How effective is cloud seeding? **No one really knows. Only clouds that are likely to produce rain are seeded, so it is impossible to tell if the rain was caused naturally or as a result of the seeding.**

QUIZ 3

Clouds

Lessons 9–12

Fill in the blank with the correct term from below.

1. Water vapor enters the atmosphere primarily through _**evaporation**_.

2. The _**water cycle**_ describes how water is reused over and over.

3. _**Precipitation**_ is water that is leaving the atmosphere.

4. When water vapor condenses in the atmosphere it forms a _**cloud**_.

5. A bubble of warm moist air is called a _**convection cell**_.

6. _**Stratus**_ clouds form in layers or sheets.

7. Big fluffy clouds are called _**cumulus**_ clouds.

8. _**Cirrus**_ clouds are wispy and curly.

9. Clouds that are likely to produce rain are called _**nimbus**_ clouds.

10. _**Hail**_ is large frozen pellets of ice falling from the atmosphere.

11. Water that crystallizes in the clouds and falls to the earth is called _**snow**_.

12. A long period without precipitation is called a _**drought**_.

13. _**Drizzle**_ is tiny droplets of water too small to be called rain.

14. All snowflakes have _**six**_ sides.

15. _**Cloud seeding**_ is sometimes used to try to produce rain.

16. Only about _**ten**_ percent of all clouds produce precipitation.

Challenge questions

Mark each statement as either True or False.

17. _F_ The water table is the surface of a lake.

18. _T_ Water flows through permeable rock.

19. _T_ Fog is a cloud that touches the ground.

20. _F_ Radiation fog occurs on windy nights.

21. _T_ Coastal areas often experience advection fog.

22. _T_ Water droplets require a condensation nucleus to coalesce.

23. _T_ Upslope fog occurs near mountains.

24. _F_ Acid rain is a myth.

25. _T_ Rain water is naturally acidic.

Storms

13 Air Masses & Weather Fronts

Creating the weather

Supply list

Empty 2-liter plastic bottle

Supplies for Challenge

Round plate or dish   Food coloring

Syrup

What did we learn?

- What is an air mass? **A large amount of air that has uniform temperature and humidity.**

- How do air masses form? **When there is very little wind in an area, the air does not move around much and becomes uniform.**

- How does the air pressure compare between warm and cold air masses? **Warm air masses usually have lower air pressure than cold air masses.**

Taking it further

- How would a cold air mass that develops over land be classified? **A continental polar air mass.**

- Why do most weather changes occur along weather fronts? **Air becomes very unsettled along a front. This allows air to heat up and cool down, which encourages precipitation. The air pressure, temperature, and humidity levels are different from one air mass to another, so when one air mass displaces another it will probably change the weather.**

14 Wind

Hold onto your hat

Supply list

Metal clothes hanger   Masking tape

Large trash bag

What did we learn?

- What is the main cause of wind? **The sun heats the earth and air. Hot air rises and cooler air moves in to take its place.**

- What is a jet stream? **A very fast moving current of air high in the atmosphere.**

- What are trade winds? **Winds that consistently blow in a particular direction in an area of the ocean during a particular season.**

Taking it further

- Why was it important for sailors of sailing ships to know about trade winds, doldrums, and other prevailing winds? **They could use the winds to help them sail faster, and they wanted to avoid the doldrums. Today's ships are not dependent on wind so this is not as big of an issue for shipping today as it used to be.**

- Why does the breeze near the coast blow toward the land in the morning and toward the sea at night? **Land heats and cools faster than water so the air above the land heats faster than the air above the water during the day and cools faster after sunset.**

15 Thunderstorms

Lightning and thunder

Supply list

Furry stuffed animal   Piece of cloth

What did we learn?

- What is a thunderstorm? **A large storm with high winds, lots of rain, thunder, and lightning.**

- What causes lightning? **Water particles and ice crystals rub against each other creating ions. Positive ions collect at the top of the cloud and negative ions collect at the bottom. When these ions connect, energy is released in the form of light.**

- What causes thunder? **Lightning heats the air, causing it to expand and then contract very quickly as it cools, which causes an explosive sound.**

Taking it further

- Why does hail form in thunderstorms that have high clouds? **Higher clouds form when the air is** moving more quickly up and down. At higher altitudes the water freezes, forming ice pellets and the faster moving air forces the pellets up into the cloud over and over, forming hail.

- Why do thunderstorms usually form on hot summer days? **The hotter the air, the more it will expand causing more updrafts and bigger clouds.**

Challenge: Flash Floods

- **Things you can do to be safe in a severe thunderstorm include: Monitor the weather station when severe storms are likely so you have as much warning as possible. Seek shelter inside a house or other building. Stay away from water. Because of the electrical nature of lightning, avoid using the telephone or taking a shower during a severe storm and do not touch metal pipes, fences, or wires. Do not stand on a hilltop; avoid being the tallest object around if you are stuck outside. Get to higher ground if a flash flood is predicted.**

16 Tornadoes

Swirling wind

Supply list

Two empty 2-liter plastic bottles

Duct tape

Plastic tornado tube connector
(optional but recommended)

What did we learn?

- What causes a tornado to develop? **Warm updrafts suck cool downdrafts into them. The falling drier air can cause the updraft to begin to spiral. If there is enough heat and energy, the spiral can tighten and speed up, resulting in a tornado.**

- What is the difference between a funnel cloud and a tornado? **A funnel cloud does not touch the ground.**

- What is a waterspout? **A tornado that develops over the water.**

- When do most tornadoes occur in the United States? **In the springtime.**

Taking it further

- How does the jet stream affect tornado formation? **The jet stream is a fast moving current of air at high altitudes. It can cause the air in a thunderstorm to move more quickly, adding energy to the storm. This encourages tornado formation.**

- Why should you take shelter during a tornado? **The greatest threat to people during a tornado is flying debris. Taking shelter can protect you from the debris.**

17 Hurricanes

Typhoons

Supply list

Copy of "Storm Word Scramble"

Storm Word Scramble

1. When warm, moist air cools. **condensation**
2. A large amount of air with uniform temperature and humidity. **air mass**
3. Where two air masses meet. **front**
4. Air movements caused by the sun heating the ground more near the equator than at the poles. **global winds**
5. A very high, fast-moving current of air. **jet stream**
6. Phenomenon caused when ions discharge energy in a cloud. **lightning**
7. A spiraling cloud that does not touch the ground. **funnel cloud**
8. A tornado that forms over water. **waterspout**
9. A hurricane that forms in the Pacific Ocean. **typhoon**
10. Rising sea level in front of a hurricane. **storm surge**
11. Equipment used by National Weather Service to predict tornadoes and hurricanes. **Doppler radar**
12. Person who studies the weather. **meteorologist**
13. Location where 90% of hurricanes form. **Pacific Ocean**
14. Type of cloud found in thunderstorms. **cumulonimbus**
15. Instrument for indicating wind direction. **wind sock**

What did we learn?

- What is a hurricane? **A huge storm that develops over warm waters.**
- Where do most hurricanes occur? **In the western Pacific Ocean.**
- What is the difference between a tropical depression, a tropical storm, and a hurricane? **Tropical depression has wind speeds of 25–38 mph; tropical storm has wind speeds of 39–73 mph; and a hurricane has wind speeds of at least 74 mph.**

Taking it further

- Why does a hurricane dissipate once it reaches land? **The storm is fueled or energized by the warm moist air of the tropical ocean. Once it reaches land, the energy to keep the storm going is no longer there.**
- How does warm water help create and energize a hurricane? **The warm water easily evaporates and the warm air rises. As it rises, the air cools and the water condenses. The condensing water releases heat causing more water to evaporate setting up a cycle that can result in hurricane formation.**

QUIZ 4 Storms

Lessons 13–17

Choose the best answer for each question or statement.

1. _B_ Most weather is determined by the location and movement of _____.
2. _A_ When two air masses meet what do they form?
3. _D_ An air mass has uniform _____.
4. _C_ Which weather phenomenon keeps temperatures more even on the earth?
5. _A_ When the wind blows from the sea to the land it is called a _____.
6. _A_ Winds that blow straight up consistently are called _____.
7. _C_ About the highest altitude that thunderstorms can reach is _____.
8. _A_ God provides a way to return nitrogen to the soil through _____.

9. _D_ A spiraling cloud that does not touch the ground is called a _____.

10. _A_ Hurricanes lose power when they _____.

11. _C_ A tropical cyclone that begins in the Northwest Pacific Ocean is called a _____.

12. _A_ The explosive sound caused by expanding and contracting air in a thunderstorm is _____.

Challenge questions

Fill in the blank with the correct term from below.

13. Scientists measure _high altitude winds_ several times a day to determine where air masses are likely to move.

14. _Mountains_ and _large lakes_ are two geological features that can affect how weather fronts move.

15. Jet streams are stronger during the _winter_ than in the _summer_.

16. Jet streams play a role in the formation of _tornadoes_.

17. You should climb to higher ground in the event of a _flash flood_.

18. _Doppler_ radar is used to determine the speed and direction that a storm is moving.

19. _Phased array_ radar will be able to scan the atmosphere much more quickly than current radar.

20. _Hurricane Hunters_ fly their airplanes through hurricanes and other storms.

21. Weather satellites allow scientists to view all of a _hurricane_ at one time.

22. _TOTO_ was a portable weather station placed in the path of a tornado.

23. A _dropsonde_ is a portable weather station dropped into a hurricane.

24. Because of the jet stream it is often faster to fly from _west_ to _east_.

Unit 5
Weather Information

18 Gathering Weather Information

What is the weather like?

Supply list

2 thermometers   Cotton cloth

Rubber band   Dish of water

Sling psychrometer (optional)

What did we learn?

- What does a meteorologist measure with a thermometer? **Temperature of the air.**
- What is air temperature? **A measure of the movement of air molecules indicating the energy they possess.**
- What are the two temperature scales commonly used? **Fahrenheit and Celsius.**
- What does a meteorologist measure with a barometer? **Air pressure.**
- What is air pressure? **The amount of pressure or force that the air exerts on the earth.**

- What does a meteorologist measure with a psychrometer? **Relative humidity.**
- What is relative humidity? **The ratio of the amount of moisture in the air to the amount of moisture the air could hold at the current temperature.**

Taking it further

- Why does a sling psychrometer give faster results than a stationary psychrometer? **The wet bulb of a sling psychrometer is exposed to dry air more quickly because of its movement, so water evaporates more quickly, giving a faster reading.**
- Why do thermometers need to be kept out of direct sunlight? **The energy from the sun will directly heat the liquid in the thermometer and will give a higher reading than the air temperature around it.**

19 More Weather Instruments

What else do they use?

Supply list

Jar with flat bottom   Tape

Ruler   Waterproof marker

What did we learn?

- How do meteorologists measure wind? **An anemometer measures wind speed and a wind sock or wind vane indicates wind direction.**

- How do meteorologists measure weather at higher altitudes? **With weather balloons carrying radiosondes—boxes with weather instruments that transmit measurements back to the weather station.**
- What sophisticated instruments do meteorologists use? **Radar, Doppler radar, satellites, and computers.**

Taking it further

- Why is it important for a meteorologist to take weather readings at higher altitudes? **This gives him/her a picture of the entire weather system. It shows the size of air masses and it shows where weather fronts are occurring.**

- Why might a weather satellite be useful for tracking a hurricane? **A satellite can show the whole storm as well as its path in relation to landmasses.**

- Why are computers necessary for weather tracking and forecasting? **The amount of data needed to understand the weather is enormous. Computers can take all of that data and analyze it and print it in formats that are easier for people to read and understand.**

20 Reporting & Analyzing Weather Information

Making it all make sense

Supply list

Copy of "Weather Station Model" worksheet

Weather Station Model worksheet

1. How much of the sky is covered with clouds? **Complete cloud cover (100%).**
2. From which direction is the wind blowing? **Southwest.**
3. What is the wind speed? **15 knots.**
4. What is the current temperature? **78°F.**
5. Is any precipitation falling? If so, what kind? **Yes, rain.**
6. What is the current dew point? **40°F.**
7. What is the current air pressure? **1015.8 millibars .**

What did we learn?

- What happens to the weather data collected at weather stations? **The information is sent to the National Weather Service where it is compiled and analyzed, and then used to generate weather charts and maps, and to make forecasts.**

- Other than from land-based weather stations, where does the National Weather Service get weather information? **From airborne radiosondes, aircraft, ships, radar, and satellites.**

- What group of the National Weather Service generates local severe thunderstorm and flash flood warnings? **Local Weather Forecasting Offices.**

Taking it further

- Why is it necessary for one location to collect and analyze all of the weather data across the United States? **Air masses change the weather as they move across the country. It is necessary to know where the different air masses are, how big they are, and in what directions they are moving. This can only be obtained by compiling measurements from multiple locations.**

- Why is a standard picture type or model needed for reporting weather information? **God designed people to be able to quickly process pictures into information, so anyone looking at the model can immediately see the weather conditions in a particular area. This is faster and easier than a written description.**

- Why must the information in the model be converted to electrical signals before it is transmitted to the National Weather Service's computer? **Computers only deal with electrical signals; pictures are for humans.**

21 Forecasting the Weather

Making predictions

Supply list

Copy of "Weather Forecasting" worksheet

Newspaper weather report

Supplies for Challenge

Graph paper   Colored pencils

What did we learn?

- How do meteorologists predict what the weather will be like? **Weather data from around the country and around the world is fed into a computer that generates weather forecasts for each area of the country. Local meteorologists use these forecasts as well as their own experience to predict what the weather will be like for the next several days.**

- What is an important function of local National Weather Service offices? **They monitor weather conditions and put out warnings and alerts when dangerous weather conditions are likely to develop.**

- Other than local weather forecasts, what types of weather forecasts are generated by the NWS? **Fire weather, airport weather (TAF), coastal weather forecast, offshore weather forecast, hurricane forecasts, and climate change forecasts.**

Taking it further

- Why are weather forecasts more accurate today than they were 20 years ago? **New computer programs are able to compile more information and make better models of the weather, plus more information is available.**

- Are weather forecasts always reliable? **No, the weather is very complicated and will never be fully understood. God is the only one who knows exactly what the weather will be.**

22 Weather Station

Collecting your own data

Final Project supply list

Copy of "Weather Data Sheet"

Clear plastic tubing   6-inch ruler

Food coloring   Soda straw

Modeling clay   Duct tape

Waterproof marker   Thin stick or skewer

String   Cardboard or tagboard

Empty bottle

Weather station with an anemometer (optional)

What did we learn?

- What does each instrument in your weather station measure? **Thermometer—temperature; psychrometer—relative humidity; wind sock—wind direction; anemometer—wind speed; barometer—air pressure; rain gauge—precipitation.**

Taking it further

- Why might you want to have your own weather station? **It's fun and educational.**

- Why might your weather readings be different from what is reported in the newspaper or on TV? **Your instruments are not as accurate and they are taking their measurements in a different location.**

- Did you see any relationship between air pressure and wind and rain? **You most likely noticed that when the air pressure changed there was more wind. Also, lower air pressure indicates a warm front that usually has more moisture and is more likely to bring rain. Higher air pressure usually indicates a cold front that is likely to have drier air and is less likely to bring rain.**

- What changes did you see in your temperature readings from day to day? **Answers will vary.**

QUIZ 5

Weather Information

Lessons 18–22

Mark each statement as either True or False.

1. _T_ A meteorologist is someone who studies the weather.

2. _F_ A barometer is used to measure temperature.

3. _F_ Air pressure goes up as you go up in altitude.

4. _T_ A psychrometer is used to measure relative humidity in the air.

5. _F_ All weather sayings are superstitious myths.

6. _T_ Meteorologists use many different instruments to understand the weather.

7. _T_ Wind direction can be shown by using a wind sock.

8. _T_ Weather satellites are very valuable tools for meteorologists.

9. _F_ Weather balloons are used to measure the weather on the ground.

10. _T_ Doppler radar can help detect severe storms more quickly than regular radar.

11. _T_ Computers are very important tools for meteorologists.

12. _F_ A weather station model is not useful for conveying information.

13. _T_ The National Weather Service helps local meteorologists make forecasts.

14. _F_ Weather forecasts were more accurate before computers were used.

15. _T_ You can collect weather data at home.

16. _F_ An anemometer shows wind direction.

17. _F_ With enough information anyone can predict the weather accurately.

18. _T_ Aircraft and ships are used to help collect weather data.

19. _T_ A rain gauge collects rain to show how much precipitation has fallen.

20. _T_ God ultimately controls the weather.

Challenge questions

Match the term with its definition.

21. _C_ Equivalent temperature if the air was dry and still

22. _B_ Calculation using temperature and relative humidity

23. _D_ Calculation using temperature and wind speed

24. _E_ Satellite stays over the same earth location

25. _A_ Satellite moves over the earth's poles

Short answer:

26. Pete is outside when the temperature is 40°F and the wind is blowing at 15 miles per hour. Polly is outside when the temperature is 30°F and the wind is blowing at 5 miles per hour. Who is likely to feel more comfortable? **Polly; Pete's apparent temp. is 22.4°F; Polly's apparent temp. is 26.9°F.**

27. Paul is outside when the temperature is 90°F and the relative humidity is 50%. Patty is outside when the temperature is 85°F and the relative humidity is 80%. Who is likely to feel more comfortable? **Paul; Paul's apparent temp. is 94.6°F; Patty's apparent temp. is 96.8°F.**

Ocean Movement

23 Overview of the Oceans
Exploring the seas

Supply list

Copy of "World Map"   Colored pencils or markers
World atlas

What did we learn?

- What are the names of the five oceans? **Pacific, Atlantic, Indian, Antarctic (or Southern), and Arctic.**
- Which ocean is the largest? **The Pacific Ocean.**
- How much of the earth is covered by the oceans? **About 71%.**

Taking it further

- How do the oceans affect the weather? **The oceans change temperature more slowly than land, so winds are generated near the ocean. Also, the heat energy in the ocean fuels many storms including hurricanes. Oceans are where most evaporation takes place so they ultimately generate most precipitation.**
- Why do some people say there is only one ocean? **All of the oceans are connected to each other so you could say there is only one ocean on earth.**
- Why was the Indian Ocean the first ocean to have established trade routes? **The monsoon winds blow steadily in one direction for half the year and then blow in the other direction the other half of the year. This made it easy for ships to sail to particular areas during certain times of the year.**

24 Composition of Seawater

Isn't it just water?

Supply list

Dark construction paper   Paint brush
Salt   Water

What did we learn?

- What are the main elements found in the ocean besides water? **Salt, magnesium, and bromine.**
- How does salt get into the ocean? **Water flowing over land dissolves salt and other minerals then leaves them behind in the oceans when the water evaporates.**
- What is one gas that is dissolved in the ocean water? **Oxygen is the main gas; nitrogen, carbon dioxide, and other gases are present as well.**

Taking it further

- Why is there more oxygen near the surface of the ocean than in deeper parts? **Phytoplankton and other plants grow near the surface and produce oxygen that dissolves in the water. Also, some oxygen dissolves into the water from the air.**
- How does the saltiness of the ocean support the idea of a young earth? **If the earth were billions of years old, the amount of salt in the oceans would be much higher than it is today. The amount of salt in the ocean is consistent with an earth about 6,000 years old.**

25 Ocean Currents

Moving around the world

Supply list

2 small bottles or jars   Red and blue food coloring
Large glass bowl

Supplies for Challenge

World map from lesson 23

What did we learn?

- What is a surface ocean current? **A continuous movement of water in a particular direction on the surface of the ocean.**
- What are the main causes of surface currents? **Heating from the sun and movement by the wind.**
- How fast do surface currents usually move? **2–3 miles per hour.**
- What is a subsurface ocean current? **A continuous movement of water in a particular direction under the surface of the ocean.**

- What are the main causes of subsurface currents? **Differences in density of warmer and cooler water and differences in density of saltier and less salty water.**

Taking it further

- What climate changes do warm surface currents cause? **Coastal areas near warm currents tend to be warmer and have milder winters.**
- What climate changes do cool surface currents cause? **Coastal areas near cool currents tend to be drier than other areas, often resulting in deserts.**
- Why do warm surface currents move away from the equator while cooler currents move toward the equator? **The sun shines more intensely at the equator so the water is warmed more there than at the poles; the wind then moves this warm water away from the equator.**

26 Waves

Gently lapping the shore

Supply list

Small and large bottle   Slinky
String

What did we learn?

- How are waves generated? **Friction between the wind and the surface of the water picks up water and moves it a short distance. This adds energy to the surface of the ocean causing it to move in waves.**
- How far does a particular water molecule move when a wave is generated? **Only a short distance, perhaps a few feet at most.**
- What is the crest of a wave? **The crest is the highest part of the wave.**

- What is the trough of a wave? **The trough is the lowest part of the wave.**
- What are two ways to measure a wave? **Wave height—the difference between the crest and the trough, and wavelength—the distance between two crests.**

Taking it further

- Explain how a wave can move across the ocean without moving the water molecules across the ocean. **The individual molecules are moved a short distance by the wind. When they fall back down to the surface of the ocean they transfer their energy to other molecules that then move forward. Those molecules hit other molecules and so on until the wave dies or reaches the shore.**

- What kind of a path does an individual water molecule take in a wave? **It is lifted by the wind, moves forward, falls down and is pushed back by other molecules—so it travels in a small circular path.**
- Why does a wave get tall as it approaches the shore? **Friction causes the base of the wave to slow down** when it hits the ocean floor. This pushes more water up, causing the wave to get taller and then break.
- Why are tsunamis such dangerous waves? **A tsunami is a wave that travels very fast and has a tremendous amount of energy. As it reaches the shore, it causes large amounts of water to pile up so that a giant wall of water hits the shore causing massive flooding.**

27 Tides

The highs and lows of the sea

Supply list

Copy of "Ocean Movements Word Search"

Ocean Movements Word Search

```
I P M C B E I Y D N E A P X Z
C B R G R A I F C E K P L U Y
U O E R I B L I M A N U S T W
R F W A V E L E N G T H T D Q
R H F V B R E A K E R F I E E
E K L I N J I E Y L O W S R
N N E T L Y R E T V U C S C E
T D E Y S W H R I K G J G R V
X T Z Y W G O U S N H V F E L
M N H T I D E L N F T V N S O
V C K H N I H U E I R I P T B
R E D S D H I J D K L D E V D
C A F E H U F R I C T I O N N
I D I E C A F R U S B U S U X
V G I J K Y T S T R U N F Q O
```

What did we learn?

- What is a high tide? **When the water level is the highest along a shore.**

- What causes the water level to change along the shore? **The gravitational pull of the moon and to a lesser extent the gravitational pull of the sun.**
- How often does a high or low tide occur each day? **There are two high tides and two low tides each day, approximately six hours apart.**

Taking it further

- Why does a spring tide only occur when there is a full moon or when there is a new moon? **This is the only time during the month when the sun is in a direct line with the earth and the moon, thus adding its gravitational pull to that of the moon.**
- Since the sun is so much larger than the moon, why doesn't it have a greater effect on the tides than the moon? **Because the moon is much closer than the sun: 240,000 miles (386,000 km) vs. 93 million miles (150 million km).**
- Where should you build your sand castle if you don't want the water to knock it down? **Farther from the water than the highest point that the waves reach during high tide.**

28 Wave Erosion

Wearing down the shore

Supply list

Paint roller pan   Empty plastic bottle

Sand

Supplies for Challenge

Copy of "Erosional Land Formations" worksheet

What did we learn?

- What causes erosion along a beach? **Waves; large waves from storms and tsunamis cause the most damage, but everyday waves cause erosion as well.**
- What are some problems that can arise from wave erosion? **The changing shoreline can cause problems**

with buildings that are built too close to the shore. Also, sand that is moved from the shore can block bays and build up sand bars that block the movement of ships.

- What features have been formed along the shore by the erosion from waves? **Sea caves, arches, and columns of stone.**

Taking it further

- Why don't shores completely erode if water is constantly pulling sand away from them? **Water is also**

bringing new sand and debris and depositing them as well.

- How can you protect your building from the damaging effects of tsunamis and other storm-generated waves? **Build further from the shore.**

Challenge: Erosional Land Formations worksheet

1. **Spit**
2. **Hook**
3. **Barrier island**
4. **Bay barrier**

29 Energy from the Ocean

Making it work for us

Supply list

The Magic School Bus on the Ocean Floor by Joanna Cole

What did we learn?

- What are three ways that people are using the ocean to generate electricity? **Tidal barrages, wave towers and wave buoys, and heat exchangers.**

Taking it further

- Why are tidal barrages used infrequently? **There are only a few places where there is a constant flow of water, and the barrages can damage the ecosystems.**

- Why do heat exchangers have to be built near the equator? **They rely on a difference in water temperature. The water that is hundreds of feet below the surface is cold no matter where you are, but the surface waters are consistently warm only in tropical areas.**

- Scientists hope to use the warm tropical waters to generate electricity. What natural weather phenomenon is fueled by these warm tropical waters? **Hurricanes, El Niño.**

QUIZ 6 Ocean Movement

Lessons 23–29

Fill in the blank with the correct term.

1. List the five oceans of the world. _**Pacific, Atlantic, Indian, Antarctic (or Southern), Arctic.**_
2. The _**monsoon**_ winds allowed trade routes to be established in the Indian Ocean.
3. The main mineral dissolved in seawater is _**salt**_.
4. There is more oxygen in the ocean near the surface because of _**algae**_ growing there.
5. The three main ways that the ocean moves are _**currents**_, _**tides**_, and _**waves**_.

6. Cold water is more _**dense**_ than warm water, so it sinks.
7. Land near cold water currents tends to have weather that is _**dry and cold**_.
8. A body of warm water in the Pacific Ocean that greatly affects weather is _**El Niño**_.
9. The highest point of a wave is called the _**crest**_.
10. The lowest point of a wave is called the _**trough**_.

Mark each statement as either True or False.

11. _F_ Water molecules are moved hundreds of miles across the ocean by waves.

12. _T_ Friction between the air and the water causes waves to form.

13. _F_ The highest part of a wave is called the trough.

14. _T_ A tsunami is a very dangerous wave.

15. _T_ Tides are a result of the gravitational pull of the moon.

16. _T_ A rip current can pull a swimmer far out to sea.

17. _F_ Erosion from waves is never harmful.

18. _T_ Movement of the ocean is beneficial for all life on earth.

Challenge questions

Choose the best answer for each question or statement.

19. _B_ What field of science began with the Challenger Expedition in 1872?

20. _A_ How many volumes of information were published after the Challenger Expedition?

21. _D_ Which is not a method of desalination?

22. _A_ Where are the majority of desalination plants located?

23. _C_ Major surface currents combine to form these five major circulations.

24. _B_ Surface currents and prevailing winds rotate counterclockwise in the northern hemisphere due to this.

25. _C_ What scale is used to describe wind and waves in the open ocean?

26. _A_ What is the difference between high tide and low tide called?

27. _D_ What is a whirlpool caused by changing tides called?

28. _C_ What erosional land formation closes off the mouth of a bay?

Unit 7
Sea Floor

30 Sea Exploration

Exploring the depths

Supply list

Deck of playing cards

What did we learn?

- What invention in the 1940s allowed divers to more freely explore the ocean? **The Aqua-Lung—a portable air tank.**
- How do oceanographers study the ocean today? **They scuba dive in relatively shallow water and they use submersibles and remotely operated vehicles to see what is in the deeper parts of the ocean.**
- What special equipment do submersibles have? **They are specially designed to withstand great water pressure. They have video cameras, manipulator arms, and** storage containers for samples. They also have communication equipment.

Taking it further

- Why does a submersible or ROV need headlights? **Below a few hundred feet (100 m), there is no sunlight and the water is very dark. Lights are needed so the scientists can see what is down there.**
- Why can't scuba divers go very deep in the ocean? **The water pressure is too great for their bodies.**
- How are submersibles similar to spacecraft? **They both provide protection to people from the surrounding environment by providing the right air pressure and by providing air to breathe. They both contain useful equipment that allows people to explore new areas.**

31 Geography of the Ocean Floor

Mountains and valleys

Supply list

Empty aquarium or other glass case
Modeling clay

Supplies for Challenge

"World Map" from lesson 23

What did we learn?

- What are the three areas of the ocean floor? **The continental shelf, the continental slope, and the abyssal plain.**
- What are some features of the abyssal plain? **There are relatively flat areas; there are seamounts, guyots, islands, and trenches.**
- What is a guyot? **An underwater mountain with a flat top.**

Taking it further

- What part of the ocean floor is most difficult to observe? **The trenches because they are so deep and have such great water pressure.**
- What do you think is the most likely cause of seamounts? **Volcanic activity is believed to cause nearly all seamounts.**

32 Ocean Zones

Visiting the different levels

Supply list

Copy of "Ocean Zones" worksheet

Crayons or colored pencils

Supplies for Challenge

Research materials on various sea creatures

Ocean Zones worksheet

A. **Sunlit zone**

B. **Twilight zone**

C. **Midnight zone**

D. **Abyss**

E. **Trench**

Plants and animals: Accept reasonable answers—see lesson for examples.

What did we learn?

- What are the five ocean zones? **Sunlit/euphotic zone, twilight/disphotic zone, midnight/aphotic zone, abyss, and trenches.**
- What zone has the most life? **The sunlit zone.**
- Where is the sunlit zone located? **Over the continental shelf, in the top 660 feet (300 m) of water.**

Taking it further

- Why is all plant life found in the sunlit zone? **Plants need sunlight to perform photosynthesis and grow, so they cannot live where no sunlight penetrates.**
- Why are so few animals found in the very deepest parts of the ocean? **The water pressure is too great for most animals. Those that can withstand the pressure must live where there is sufficient food.**

33 Vents & Smokers

Underwater volcanoes?

Supply list

Paper

Colored pencils or markers

What did we learn?

- What is a deep-sea vent? **An area on the sea floor where very hot water shoots up from below the surface of the ocean floor.**
- What provides the food source for the animals living near these vents? **A type of bacteria that thrives on the sulfur in the vent water.**

Taking it further

- Why were scientists so surprised to find an ecosystem thriving near the deep-sea vents? **They believed that all life in the sea depended on the plants growing in the sunlit zone, but this ecosystem gets its food supply from the bacteria that grow in the hot water.**
- Why can the water stay so hot near the vents without turning to steam? **The great pressure of the water at the depths in which the vents are found keeps the water in liquid form even at very high temperatures.**

34

Coral Reefs

Animal-made islands

Supply list

Modeling clay

What did we learn?

- What is a coral? **A tiny animal that resembles an upside down jellyfish that lives in the ocean and secretes a hard cup around itself.**

- What is a coral reef? **A large collection of coral all growing together.**

- What are the three types of coral reefs? **Fringing reef, barrier reef, and atoll.**

Taking it further

- Why are coral reefs only found in relatively shallow ocean water? **The algae inside the coral require sunlight to make food.**

- Why might a coral reef be a hazard to ships? **A coral reef may not be visible from the surface but may be big enough to cause damage to the ship.**

- What could happen to a coral reef if the water became cloudy or too warm for the algae to survive? **The algae would die and the coral may eventually die as well.**

QUIZ 7

Sea Floor

Lessons 30–34

1. Label the features of the ocean floor in the following diagram.

   A. **Continent**   E. **Abyssal plain**

   B. **Continental shelf** F. **Island**

   C. **Continental slope** G. **Guyot**

   D. **Seamount**   H. **Trench**

Below, label each ocean zone. Write each plant or animal from the list below next to the zone in which you are most likely to find it.

2. 0 to 660 feet is the _sunlit (or euphotic)_ zone. **Shark, algae, coral, jellyfish, seaweed**

3. 660 to 3,300 feet is the _twilight (or disphotic)_ zone. **Octopus, bioluminescent fish, sponges**

4. 3,300 to 13,200 feet is the _midnight (or aphotic)_ zone. **Tubeworms, anglerfish, sea spider**

5. 13,200 feet and deeper is called the _abyss_. **Sea lilies**

6. Very deep canyons are called _trenches_. **No plants or animals listed**

Challenge questions

Mark each statement as either True or False.

7. _F_ Astronauts primarily study conditions under the ocean.

8. _T_ Researchers can live in the Aquarius underwater lab for long periods of time.

9. _T_ Researchers in Aquarius must undergo a decompression period before surfacing.

10. _T_ Ocean trenches are found in subduction zones.

11. _F_ Ocean trenches and ridges are found in the same areas.

12. _T_ The Mariana Trench is the lowest place on Earth.

13. _F_ Most volcanic activity takes place on land.

14. _T_ Ocean vents are usually located near underwater volcanoes.

15. _F_ Coral reefs are proven to be hundreds of thousands of years old.

16. _T_ Coral reefs can grow very rapidly.

Our Weather & Water

Lessons 1–34

Fill in the blank with the correct term from below.

1. _Meteorology_ is the study of the earth's atmosphere.

2. _Climate_ is the average weather conditions in an area over a long period of time.

3. The earth's atmosphere is 78% _nitrogen_ and 21% _oxygen_.

4. The Genesis Flood set up environmental conditions just right for an _ice age_.

5. A _glacier_ can form when snow does not completely melt in the summer.

6. Water vapor that condenses in the air forms _clouds_.

7. Water that falls from the sky is called _precipitation_.

8. The _sun_ is responsible for most of the winds we experience on earth.

9. Hurricanes can only form near the _equator_.

10. The _computer_ is the most important piece of equipment for analyzing weather.

11. Weather fronts form where two _air masses_ meet.

Analyze the weather station model and fill in the blanks.

12. Temperature: **32°F**

13. Wind speed: **15 knots**

14. Wind direction: **North**

15. Precipitation: **Snow**

16. Cloud cover: **100%**

17. Air pressure: **1020.1 millibars**

Mark each statement as either True or False.

18. _F_ Relative humidity is the total amount of water vapor in the air.

19. _T_ Meteorologists use computers to help them forecast the weather.

20. _T_ The oceans play an important role in the weather.

21. _F_ El Niño is a wind in South America.

22. _T_ The ocean contains many minerals and gases in addition to water.

23. _T_ Ocean currents are sometimes a result of different amounts of salt in the water.

24. _T_ Energy from waves can be used to make electricity.

25. _F_ Waves are always helpful.

26. _F_ Tides are lower when the sun and the moon line up.

27. _F_ Most plants and animals are found in the twilight zone of the ocean.

Match the term with its definition.

28. _B_ Very deep valley in the ocean floor

29. _E_ Very hot water coming up through sea floor

30. _C_ Large collection of colonies of polyps

31. _H_ Vehicle for deep-sea exploration

32. _F_ Animal that can glow in the dark

33. _A_ Largest ocean on earth

34. _G_ Organism that produces most of the oxygen in the ocean

35. _D_ Strong current moving water from the shore to the open sea

36. _I_ Area where most plants and animals live in the ocean

Challenge questions

37. Use the following words to label the diagram of the atmosphere with the correct levels:

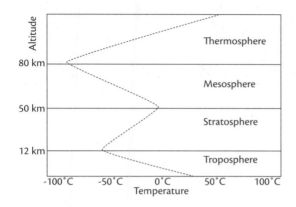

Short answer:

38. What are the four "ingredients" needed to make weather? **Earth, water, air, and sun.**

39. Explain how we get clues to what the climate was like in the past. **We get clues from fossils. The types of plants and animals found in an area can give us clues as to what the climate must have been like in order for those plants and animals to have lived there.**

40. List three kinds of fog. **Radiation, advection, steam, valley, upslope.**

41. What are two ways that acid rain can form? **Naturally—carbon dioxide in the atmosphere dissolves to create carbonic acid; chemically—sulfur and nitrogen compounds enter the air through pollution and dissolve in the water vapor to form sulfuric acid and nitric acid.**

42. The jet stream is most affected by the difference in temperature between which areas of the world? **Equator and the Poles.**

43. Name two kinds of radar that are used to detect severe weather. **Doppler, phased array.**

44. Explain how someone outside in the winter could feel more comfortable in a colder temperature than he or she does when the outside temperature is warmer. **The wind makes it feel colder because it increases the rate at which sweat evaporates, so if the wind is blowing more on a warmer day you could actually feel colder than if it blowing less on a colder day.**

45. What are two methods for desalinating ocean water. **Distillation, reverse osmosis.**

46. Do ocean ridges form where tectonic plates are moving toward each other or away from each other? **Away.**

Conclusion

Appreciating our weather and water

Supply list

Bible

Resource Guide

Many of the following titles are available from Answers in Genesis (www.AnswersBookstore.com).

Suggested Books

Weather and the Bible by Donald B. DeYoung—One hundred questions on weather-related topics are answered from the Christian perspective

Life in the Great Ice Age by Michael and Beverly Oard—Learn what life was like during the Ice Age after the Flood in this colorful novel

The New Weather Book by Michael Oard—From the practical to the pretty amazing, this book gives essential details into understanding what weather is, how it works, and how other forces impact it

The Ocean Book by Frank Sherwin—You'll be amazed by what lies beneath the surface of the world's oceans!

The Magic School Bus on the Ocean Floor by Joanna Cole—fun and informative book

The Magic School Bus Inside a Hurricane by Joanna Cole—fun way to learn about storms

Frozen in Time by Michael Oard—explanation of woolly mammoth finds

Suggested Videos

Newton's Workshop by Moody Institute—Excellent Christian science series; several titles to choose from

Global Warming—A documentary from Answers in Genesis on the science and politics surrounding global warming

Awesome Forces of God's Creation—three-DVD set from Moody, includes *Roaring Waters*, *Thundering Earth*, and *Whirling Winds*

Field Trip Ideas

- Creation Museum in Petersburg, Kentucky
- Check if your area power company has wind generating equipment; set up a tour
- Beach (if one is nearby)
- Local weather station
- Visit a scuba diving school

Creation Science Resources

Answers Book for Kids Four volumes by Ken Ham with Cindy Malott—Answers children's frequently asked questions

The New Answers Books 1–4 by Ken Ham and others—Answers frequently asked questions

The Amazing Story of Creation by Duane T. Gish—Gives scientific evidence for the creation story

Creation Science by Felice Gerwitz and Jill Whitlock—Unit study focusing on creation

Creation: Facts of Life by Gary Parker—Comparison of the evidence for creation and evolution

The Young Earth by John D. Morris—Lots of facts disproving old-earth ideas

Learn more about the Ice Age at the Kids section of the Answers in Genesis website at answersingenesis.org/kids/ice-age.

Master Supply List

The following table lists all the supplies used for *God's Design for Heaven & Earth: Our Weather & Water* activities. You will need to look up the individual lessons in the student book to obtain the specific details for the individual activities (such as quantity, color, etc.). The letter *c* denotes that the lesson number refers to the challenge activity. Common supplies such as colored pencils, construction paper, markers, scissors, tape, etc., are not listed.

Supplies needed (see lessons for details)	Lesson
Aquarium or other empty case	31
Baking dish	4
Balloons	3
Bible	35
Bottle with lid	22, 28
Candle	2
Cotton balls	11
Dry ice	10c
Duct tape	16, 22
Flour	12
Food coloring	4, 13, 22, 25
Global warming articles	8
Gloves	10c
Graph paper	2c, 21c
House plant	6
Ice	10
Jar with lid	2, 3c, 10, 19, 25, 26, 28
Masking tape	3, 4, 14, 19, 26
Matches	2, 11c
Metal clothes hanger	14
Mirror	6
Modeling clay	2, 22, 29, 31, 34

Supplies needed (see lessons for details)	Lesson
Newspaper	1, 5, 21
Paint roller pan	28
pH testing paper (optional)	12c
Piece of cloth	15, 18
Plastic bottle (empty, 2-liter)	11c, 13, 16, 22, 26
Plastic grocery bag	3c
Plastic tornado tube (optional but recommended)	16
Plastic tubing (clear)	22
Plastic zipper bag	10
Playing cards	30
Poster board/tagboard	22
Rubber band	18
Salt	24
Sand	19, 28
Shoe box	10c
Short ruler (6-inch)	22
Sling psychrometer (optional)	18
Slinky	26
Straw	22
String	3, 12, 22, 26
Stuffed animal	15
Styrofoam cups	4
Syrup	13
The Magic School Bus on the Ocean Floor	29
Thermometer	18
Trash bag (large)	14
Weather station (optional)	22
Wooden stick (small, skewer-like)	22
World atlas/map	5, 23
Yard stick/meter stick	3

Works Cited

"Acid Rain." http://www.epa.gov/acidrain/index.html.

Ardley, Neil. *The Science Book of Weather*. San Diego: Gulliver Books, 1992.

"Ashkelon Desalination Plane, Seawater Reverse Osmosis (SWRO) Plant, Israel." http://www.water-technology.net/projects/israel/.

"Benjamin Franklin." http://web.lemoyne.edu/~giunta/franklin.html.

Brice, Tim. "Heat Index." http://www.srh.noaa.gov/elp/wxcalc/heatindex.shtml.

"California's Rocky Intertidal Zones." http://ceres.ca.gov/ceres/calweb/coastal/rocky.html.

Cobb, Allan B. *Weather Observation Satellites*. New York: Rosen Publishing Group, 2003.

"Colorado Remembers Big Thompson Canyon Flash Flood of 1976." http://www.noaanews.noaa.gov/stories/s688.htm.

Conjecture Corp. "What is the Jet Stream?" http://www.wisegeek.com/what-is-the-jet-stream.htm.

Coutsoukis, Photius. "Russian Climate." http://www.photius.com/countries/russia/climate/russia_climate_climate.html.

Daly, John L. "The El Niño Southern Oscillation." http://www.john-daly.com/elnino.htm.

Demarest, Chris L. *Hurricane Hunters! Rides on the Storm*. New York: Margaret K. McElderry Books, 2006

DeYoung, Donald B. *Weather & the Bible*. Grand Rapids: Baker Book House, 1996.

"El Niño Warm Water Pool Decreasing." http://visibleearth.nasa.gov/view_rec.php?id=542.

Fleisher, Paul. *Coral Reef*. New York: Benchmark Books, 1998.

"Fog." http://www.bbc.co.uk/weather/features/understanding/fog.shtml.

Fredericks, Anthony D. *Exploring the Oceans—Science Activities for Kids*. Golden: Fulcrum Resources, 1998.

Gardiner, Brian. *Energy Demands*. London: Gloucester Press, 1990.

Gardner, Robert. *Science Project Ideas About Rain*. Berkely Heights: Enslow Publishers, Inc., 1997.

Gibbons, Gail. *Exploring the Deep, Dark Sea*. Boston: Little, Brown and Company, 1999.

Gray, Susan H. *Coral Reefs*. Minneapolis: Compass Point Books, 2001.

Harper, Suzanne. *Clouds: From Mares Tails to Thunderheads*. New York: Franklin Watts, 1997.

Haslam, Andrew, and Barbara Taylor. *Make It Work Weather*. Chicago: World Book, 1997.

"Intertidal Zones." http://neptune.spaceports.com/~marine/life.html.

Jones, Lorraine. *Super Science Projects About Weather and Naturals Forces*. New York: Rosen Central, 2000.

"Joseph Priestly, The King of Serendipity." http://home.nycap.rr.com/useless/priestly/priestly.html.

Kahl, Jonathan D. *Storm Warning: Tornadoes and Hurricanes*. Minneapolis: Lerner Publications Co., 1993

Lambert, David. *Weather*. New York: Franklin Watts, 1983.

Low, Anne Marie. "Dust Bowl Diary." http://chnm.gmu.edu.

Meltzer, Milton. *Benjamin Franklin The New American*. New York: Franklin Watts, 1988.

Mulfinger, George, and Donald E. Snyder. *Earth Science for Christian Schools*. Greenville: Bob Jones University Press, 1995.

National Wildlife Federation. *Wild About Weather*. Philadelphia: Chelsea House Publishers, 1997.

"New Detection System Listens for Tornadoes." *Windsor Tribune*. 27 May 2003.

Oard, Michael. "Human-caused Global Warming Slight So Far." http://www.answersingenesis.org/articles/aid/v1/n1/human-caused-global-warming.

Oard, Michael, and Beverly Oard. *Life in the Great Ice Age*. Colorado Springs: Master Books, 1993.

Oard, Michael. *The Weather Book*. Green Forest: Master Books, 2000.

"Ocean Currents." http://seawifs.gsfc.nasa.gov/OCEAN_PLANET/HTML/oceanography_currents_1.html.

"Ocean Exploration and Undersea Research Hydrothermal Vents." http://www.research.noaa.gov/oceans/t_vents.html.

Oxlade, Chris. *Weather*. Austin: Raintree Steck-Vaughn, 1999.

"Quick Bits of 'L.'" *Tidbits*. 8 October 2003: 2.

"Saltwater Desalination in California." http://www.coastal.ca.gov/desalrpt/dchap1.html.

Sands, Stella. "Tornadoes." *Kids Discover*. June/July 1996: 1–20.

Scher, Linda. "Hurricanes." *Kids Discover*. June 2002: 1–20.

Seibert, Patricia. *Discovering El Nino*. Brookfield: Millbrook Press, 1999.